Miles of Smiles

ALSO BY CAROLE TERWILLIGER MEYERS

• • • • • • • • • • • • •

San Francisco Family Fun

Weekend Adventures for City-Weary People: Overnight Trips in Northern California

Eating Out with the Kids in San Francisco and the Bay Area

How to Organize a Babysitting Cooperative and Get Some Free Time Away from the Kids

Getting in the Spirit: Annual Bay Area Christmas Events

Eating Out with the Kids in the East Bay

Miles of Smiles

101 GREAT CAR GAMES & ACTIVITIES

CAROLE TERWILLIGER MEYERS

Illustrated by VICTORIA CARLSON

Published by: CAROUSEL PRESS
               P.O. Box 6038
               Berkeley, CA 94706-0038
               (510) 527-5849
               info@carousel-press.com
               www.carousel-press.com

Distributed to the book trade by Publishers Group West

Library of Congress Cataloging-in-Publication Data

Meyers, Carole Terwilliger.
    Miles of smiles: 101 great car games & activities / Carole
Terwilliger Meyers.
           p.   cm.
    Includes bibliographical references.
    Summary: A collection of 101 games and activities for children and
adults to share while traveling.
    ISBN 10: 0-917120-11-6
    ISBN 13: 978-0-917120-11-4
    1. Games for travelers--Juvenile literature.   [1. Games for
travelers.   2. Games.]   1. Title.
IN PROCESS   91-45885
794--dc20   CIP
                                            AC

Manufactured in the United States of America
15 14 13 12

To my dear friend Jeff,

who invented the "Quiet Game" for my noisy children

This is a collection of the best car games and activities that I have been able to find. Most of them were not invented by me. The origin of most of them is impossible to document. Where my research has made it clear whom to credit, I have named a game's inventor in italics at the end of that game's directions. But in most cases I have become acquainted with a game through a variety of sources, and I have seen it described in a variety of ways and given a variety of titles. I welcome information regarding the original source of any game or activity described. Once verified, I will give proper credit in a future printing of this book.

CONTENTS

• • • • • • • •

Page numbers are in parentheses.

INTRODUCTION FOR PARENTS

· · · · · · · · · · · · · · · ·

We all know how tedious and boring certain aspects of travel can become—with or without children. You know . . . when you've been driving down that straight, hot two-lane highway through the desert for several hours . . . or when you're waiting at the airport for a delayed flight . . . or when you're stuck in a cramped cabin waiting to disembark a cruise ship. I'm sure you can think of plenty more examples.

But these times don't have to be tedious and boring. With the entertaining games and activities in this book—kept handy in your glove compartment, carry-on, pocket, or purse—you can save the day. Quicker than an adolescent can protest about going along on a family vacation, you'll have your family involved in an interesting way to pass the time.

And speaking of adolescents, who can sometimes be less than enthusiastic about doing anything a parent might suggest, consider converting points to money as an incentive for them to participate. Enthusiasm has been known to bubble over when the possibility of financial gain is offered—especially if a teenager gets to win while the parent loses. This is a fairly sure and harmless way to get teens to participate as willingly as they did when they were younger.

Most of the games and activities included in this book appeal to all ages. Those that don't can, with minor adjustments, be made to appeal to all ages . . . or to particular ages. (See page 120 for age recommendations.) Fine-tune the games and activities to make them perfect for your unique family. For instance, in games that gradually eliminate players you may prefer to charge penalty points to the losers if you have only two players, or if you want to keep everyone participating. Or you may want to play as a group, with all wins being group wins. The possibilities are limited only by your imagination.

Although many games and activities are specific to car travel, most can be adapted and played anywhere your family finds itself bored—in a bus, train, plane, or ship, even in a restaurant or a doctor's waiting room.

This book has been designed so that you can pick a game or activity by subject, by title, or by just selecting a number between 1 and 101 and taking potluck. Ninety-seven may be played using just your minds and mouths. However, when you have a pencil handy you can elaborate on many of the games by having your kids actually write down answers—giving them an opportunity to practice their penmanship and spelling. In the games and activities where players are asked if they can think of more words or examples, they can actually write them down for future reference. And when you have crayons or felt pens along, you may want to let your children color in the illustrations. You will need to read the rules to younger children, but those age 7 and older can probably read on their own.

Note that when playing in a car, I recommend that you do not include the driver in most games and activities. But do consider using your odometer for counting out a particular number of miles to signal the end of a game.

Finally, in the effort to avoid using exclusionary language, I have sometimes resorted to using "they" as a singular pronoun. Though we all use it in ordinary conversation, we're not accustomed to seeing it in print. It seemed the best solution here, however, because these pages will often be read aloud.

Games & Activities

BUS STOP

• • • • • •

One player counts the number of people spotted waiting at bus stops outside one side of the car. The other player does the same on the other side. The first to count 100 people wins.

A variation of this game permits the players to count together.

2 MIND YOUR Ps AND Qs

· · · · · · · · · · ·

Each player looks for Ps and Qs on signs, license plates, etc. A particular P and Q may be counted only by the first player to see it. The player who has counted the largest number of Ps and Qs when the game is over is the winner. Set a specific time or mileage limit.

3 TWO-DOOR, FOUR-DOOR

· · · · · · · · · · ·

In this game one player looks for two-door cars while the other player looks for four-door cars. Set a limit (25, 50, 100) and start counting. The first player to reach the limit is the winner.

4 WHAT AM I COUNTING?

· · · · · · · · · · · ·

One player silently selects for counting a category of objects that may be viewed outside the car. With very young children, broad categories such as Trucks, Telephone Poles, or Cows work well. With older children, more specific categories such as Pink Houses or White Horses work better. As the car passes a selected object, the player counts out loud, adding to their total. The other players try to guess what is being counted. The first player to guess correctly becomes the next counter.

5 YOUR NEW CAR
· · · · · · · · · ·

In this pretending game, each player is promised a new car. To find out what kind it is, the first player picks any number and then all the players count together the cars passing in the opposite direction until the number is reached. The car that is seen when the players reach the goal number is the player's "pretend" new car.

A variation of this game is to have players look for their numbers on the license plates of passing cars. The first one to find their number is also the first one to know what their pretend new car will be. That person then helps the others.

6 LICENSE PLATE ALPHABET
. . . .

Each player looks for the letters of the alphabet, in order, on license plates. The first player to find them all wins. If one license plate has more than one needed letter, each letter may be used if they are in consecutive order. For example, if players are at D and spot a plate with **EFJ** on it, they may use both the E and the F. But if players spot a plate with **EJF**, they may use only the E. This game may be played with everyone calling out their letters as they spot them, or silently, with no one saying anything until they have completed their alphabet.

A variation of this game requires doing the alphabet backwards. Another variation that works well with two players is to have one player look for the letters A through I and have the other look for the numbers 1 through 9.

7 LICENSE PLATE COUNTING

• • • • • • • • • • • • • •

Players begin by looking for the number 1 on a license plate. When found, they look for 2. And so on. The game becomes more difficult when players reach double-digit numbers and the number must appear as consecutive digits. (For example, when looking for 23, a plate numbered AFR**23**9 is acceptable, but AFR**25**3 is not.) To end the game, pick either a number goal (50, 100, 200, etc.) or a time limit.

Players may participate as individuals, as teams, or all together. If they all work together, numbers must be said out loud as they are found. If they play as individuals, there is the option of keeping track of the numbers silently.

LICENSE PLATE MATH

. . . .

Using license plates, the first player gives a math problem to the second player. For example, the first player might say, "Add together the first two numbers on the license plate on the car in front of ours." Or "Add up all the individual digits." Or "Multiply the first digit by the last digit." And so on. The second player receives one point for a correct answer, no points for a wrong answer, and then gives a math problem to the next player.

To make the game harder, use double-digit numbers. Or stretch out the problem by asking the player to do a second function, such as subtracting the second number on the license plate of the car behind yours from the answer arrived at for the first part of the problem.

9 LICENSE PLATE PALINDROMES
• • • • • • •

Palindromes are words or numbers that read the same backwards as forward. For example, *pop* or *323*. A player gets a point for being the first to spot a palindrome on a license plate.

10 LICENSE PLATE PHRASES
• • • • • • • • • • • • •

In this game the players select a passing car. Using the letters on its license plate, they make up a phrase beginning with those letters. For example, **SSF** could be **S**o **S**o **F**unny while **RBS** could be **R**ed **B**irds **S**creech. After players have worked together on these phrases for awhile, have them figure out their own phrases.

It's fun to require the phrases to be silly.

11 LICENSE PLATE ROULETTE
· · · · · · · · · · · ·

Each player starts with 25 points. Players then make bets on what the last digit of the license plate number will be on the next car to pass. Players may wager up to the number of points they have left. Winners gain the number of points they wagered; losers lose the number of points they wagered. A player with no points left is out. The last remaining player wins.

A game might go like this: The first player wagers 3 points that the number will be 5. The second player wagers 4 points that the number will be 4. The number is 5, so the first player wins. The first player gains 3 points and the second player loses 4 points. If the number had been anything other than 5 or 4, both players would have had to subtract points from their scores (the first player would subtract 3; the second player would subtract 4).

12 LICENSE PLATE SPELLING

Randomly pick a license plate. Using the letters only, and in the same sequence as spotted, see who can spell the longest word. For example, if the license plate reads **TRP**, a short word might be **TR**i**P**, a longer word **T**a**RP**oon.

You can make the game easier by not requiring that letters be used in the same sequence.

A variation of this game is to have each player pick a word with the same number of letters. They then look for the letters in sequential order on passing license plates. For example, if the word is *vacation*, the V must be found first, then the A, and so on. The first player to find the last letter of his or her word wins.

13 ALPHABETS
· · · · · · ·

Players take turns naming items in a particular category in alphabetical order. For example, if the category is Foods, the first player names a food beginning with the letter A, the second player names a food beginning with the letter B, and so on. The game is over when you finish Z.

Alter the game to name only desserts. Or only "yucky" foods. And so on. Suggestions for more categories are on page 112.

Make the game more difficult by requiring players to repeat all the previous items mentioned before adding a new one.

14 ANTONYMS
· · · · · · ·

The first player names a word. The other players try to name its antonym, or opposite. Then the second player names a word. And so on. Here are some words to get you started:

clean	imaginary	healthy
funny	shout	brave
polite	ambitious	humble
borrow	enormous	interior
obese	relaxed	walk
wrinkled	simple	summer

Can you think of more antonyms?

15 BACKWARDS SPELLING BEE

One player thinks of a travel-related word and spells it backwards. The other player mentally transposes it and then says it out loud. If more than one player is transposing, the first one to say the word correctly wins. Start with short words, especially when young children are playing. Then progress to longer words.

Here are some words to get you thinking:

car	gas	trip
map	toll	road

16 CATEGORIES

. . . .

Players agree on a category such as Flowers. Then round-robin style each person names a type of flower, continuing until no one is able to think of a new type. In listing flowers you might come up with the obvious, such as roses, daisies, and violets, as well as the less obvious, such as begonias and cosmos. Someone who mentions a flower the others aren't familiar with, must also provide a description. Most likely you'll find yourselves pointing out these unfamiliar flowers to each other later as you notice them in your travels. Suggestions for more categories are on page 112.

Make this game harder by requiring players to use alphabetical order.

17 COMPOUND WORDS
· · · · · · · · · · · ·

A compound word combines two short words into one longer new word. In this activity the first player names a compound word—for example, *lighthouse*. The next player takes the last part of the word (*house*) and adds another word to make a new compound word. Add *boat* to form *houseboat*, for example. The game continues until the players run out of words.

18 EUPHEMISMS

Euphemisms are new, less direct words that are used to make something seem less distasteful or offensive. Here are a few examples.

OLD TERM	NEW TERM
prison	correctional facility
garbage collector	sanitary engineer
used	previously owned
Department of War	Department of Defense
died	passed away
cop	peace officer
housewife	domestic engineer
haunted	psychologically impacted
difficult	challenging
free labor	intern
no kids allowed	well-behaved children welcome

Can you think of more euphemisms?

19

FIVE Ws
· · · · · ·

When reporting a story, journalists are taught to always include the five Ws: who, what, when, where, and why. For this game one player silently selects a noun (a "what" word). For instance, the word *ball.* The others then ask the five Ws in sequence.

"*Who* would use it?"
The answer might be, "A professional baseball player."
"*What* would it be used for?"
The answer might be, "To hit."
"*When* would it be used?"
The answer might be, "In a game."

Continue until the word is guessed.

20 HOMONYMS
. . . .

Homonyms are words that sound alike but have different spellings and meanings. The first player names a homonym, then spells it and uses it in a sentence. The next player does the same with that word's mate. Here are some homonyms to get you started.

TWO-WORD HOMONYMS

bare/bear
brake/break
incite/insight
knight/night
right/write
sea/see
son/sun
tail/tale

THREE-WORD HOMONYMS

aye/eye/I
cite/sight/site
dew/do/due
pair/pare/pear
peak/peek/pique
their/there/they're
to/too/two

How many more homonyms can you think of?

Here's a game to play with the new homonyms you think of. One player silently chooses a pair of homonyms, for example *bare* and *bear*. The player then uses each word in a sentence, replacing it with the word *homonym* or any other word everyone agrees on. For example, "I went to my cupboard and it was *homonym*," and "Goldilocks was surprised to find a *homonym* in her bed." The player who guesses the correct words is next.

21

THE MINISTER'S CAT

· · · · · · · · · · · · ·

Players take turns in a specific order. The first player starts by saying, "The minister's cat is an _____ cat," filling in the blank with an adjective beginning with A. For example, "The minister's cat is an *annoying* cat." The next player repeats the sentence, substituting in another adjective beginning with A. Continue until someone either repeats an adjective or can't think of a new one. When this happens, everyone else gets a point, and the game continues using the next letter in the alphabet.

A harder variation of this game requires that all adjectives be negative. Then the cat can't be *agreeable* or *amiable*—only *angry* or *awful*.

NOW STARRING
"THE MINISTER'S CAT"

22 MULTIPLE MEANINGS

· · · · · · · · · · ·

Each of the following words has more than one meaning. The first player makes up a complete sentence using one meaning of the word. The second player makes up a complete sentence using the word's other meaning.

band	firm	nag	rare	smart
bluff	flatter	negative	relative	sock
box	fly	novel	riddle	spring
braces	hit	pen	rock	stand
cabinet	interest	pick	roll	store
cast	jar	pitch	run	strike
chop	lean	play	shake	taste
craft	might	pop	sharp	train
fire	mind	race	shell	tug

Can you think of more words with multiple meanings?

23 NOISES
· · · · · ·

Either together or taking turns, players name things that could make a particular noise. Here are some noises to get you started.

click	fizz	slurp	gurgle	splash
thump	tick-tock	roar	plunk	plop
crack	hoot	ring	boom	howl

Can you think of more noises?

24 PIG LATIN

Most children quickly learn this playful code language derived from ordinary English. Words are formed by moving the first consonant or consonant cluster of each word to the end of the word and adding the sound "ay." For instance, "Speak Pig Latin." would translate as "Eakspay Igpay Atinlay." When there is a vowel at the beginning of a word, leave it there but still add "ay" to the end. For instance, "Are we there yet?" would be, "Areay eway erethay etyay?" Set a time limit for how long everyone will try to carry on conversation in Pig Latin.

25

SIMILES
· · · · ·

Similes are figures of speech in which one thing is likened to another. Play this game by having one player say a simile, leaving out either the first or last word. Another player completes it. Here are some to get you started.

1. (Fit) as a (fiddle).
2. (Happy) as a (lark).
3. (Stubborn) as a (mule).
4. (Busy) as a (bee).
5. (Quiet) as a (mouse).

How many more of these colorful expressions can you think of?

The Silent Family

26 SPELLING BASEBALL (or GHOST)

In this word-building game the first player names the first letter of a potential word. The next player adds a letter. And so on. The object is to get one of the other players to complete a word, because the first player to complete the spelling of a word gets a strike. Then a new round begins with the second player and a new letter.

Players must have a word in mind at all times, because any player may challenge the previous player if they think no word can be formed from the letters. A player who is challenged and has no word in mind gets a strike. A player who gets three strikes is out. The game continues until only one player is left.

This game is also known as "Ghost." In Ghost, players who complete a word are given a letter from the word g-h-o-s-t. When a player has spelled out ghost, he or she "disappears."

A more difficult variation of this game allows play to continue, even though a word has been completed and a player has been given a strike, if another player has a longer word in mind. For example, if a player strikes out with *honest* and the next player had in mind *honestly* and wanted to use it to strike out the next player, they could do so.

27 SUPERLATIVES
· · · · · · · · ·

Superlatives are words that refer to something that is superior to, or excels over, all others. Here are some examples and some questions for you to answer.

There is no right or wrong answer to this first group of questions. Each person is entitled to their own opinion.

1. What is the **prettiest** thing you have ever seen?
2. What is the **ugliest** thing you have ever seen?
3. What is the **smallest** thing you have ever seen?
4. What is the **biggest** thing you have ever seen?
5. What is the **noisiest** thing you have ever heard?
6. What is the **quietest** thing you have ever heard?
7. Who is the **most beautiful** person you have ever seen?

The following questions do have right and wrong answers. Do you know the right answers?

1. What is the **deepest** lake in the United States?
2. What is the **longest** river in the United States?
3. What is the **longest** river in Europe?
4. What is the **longest** river in the world?
5. What is the **largest** body of fresh water in the world?
6. Where is the **windiest** and **foggiest** place on the West Coast of the United States?
7. Which state has the **wettest** climate in the United States?
8. Which is the **most populous** state in the United States?
9. Where is the **lowest** point in the United States?
10. What is the **smallest** state in the United States?

(Answers are on page 113.)

For more superlatives, see the Superlative Geography Quiz on page 72.
Can you think of even more superlatives?

SYNONYMS

Synonyms are words that have similar meanings. In this game the first player names a word for which they can think of a synonym. The other players take turns trying to name as many synonyms for it as possible. For example, a player might name *good*. The other players might then say *excellent, superb, outstanding,* and so on. The game continues until players run out of words.

29 TASTY TALK

Each player names a food that is sweet. Continue until you run out of ideas. Then name foods that are

> sour
> salty
> bitter
> bland
> yucky
> yummy

30 THREE-LETTER WORDS

The first player picks a three-letter word such as *hot*. The second player must then say a three-letter word starting with the last letter of *hot* — for example *ton*. The third player must then say a three-letter word starting with N. And so on. A player who can't think of a word or repeats a word is out.

31 TRAVEL SENTENCES

• • • • • • • • • • •

Each player in turn picks a destination and then makes a sentence using a mode of transportation and an activity that both begin with the same letter.

Examples are:

"I'm going to **Alaska** on an **antelope** to **ask some questions**."
"I'm going to **London** on a **lion** to **look for Lenore**."
"I'm going to **Canada** in a **car** to **catch fish**."
"I'm going to **Nevada** on a **newt** to be **nearer to Norma**."

Make this game more difficult by requiring the players to proceed in alphabetical order.

32 WORD ASSOCIATIONS
· · · · · · · · · · ·

The first player names a noun. The second player names a word associated with that noun. For example, the first player might say *salt*. The second player might answer with *pepper*. The association is obvious—both are food seasonings—and the second player gets one point.

If the second player should pick a less obvious association by using perhaps *money*, the first player may challenge. If challenged, the second player must be able to give a good reason for their answer. The second player might say, "As in salting away some money." If everyone agrees that this explanation is acceptable, then the second player gets two points, while the first player, the unsuccessful challenger, loses two points.

The next player takes the word the second player named, in this case either *pepper* or *money*, and continues the game.

33 CAREERS

· · · · · · ·

One player thinks of a word naming a career and gives the others the first and last letter. The other players each take turns asking questions about the career until someone is ready to guess the correct career. If the player guesses right, they pick the next career. If wrong, they are out of that round. Can the winner describe the kind of work done by people in that particular occupation?

Here are some career suggestions to get you started:

doctor	architect	fireman
artist	plumber	salesman
journalist	entertainer	mechanic
chef	teacher	bus driver
chauffeur	waitress	pilot

Can you name more careers?

34 ESENCES

· · · · · · ·

In this guessing game players use intuition, imagination, and logic to come up with the answer. The game begins with all players agreeing on the type of person they will work with: a famous person, a fictional character, or someone everyone in the group knows personally. Then the first player silently selects a person, and the others work to identify that person by determining his or her "essence." Players may guess at any time. Questions continue until someone guesses the right answer. For example:

First player: I am thinking of a famous person who is female.

Any player: What music is this person? First player: Mournful, hopeful music.

Any player: What kind of animal is this person? First player: A perky puppy.

Any player: What color is this person? First player: Blue.

Any player: What article of clothing is this person? First player: A gingham pinafore.

Any player: What kind of tree is this person? First player: A tree broken by a cyclone.

Any player: It's Dorothy from *The Wizard of Oz!* First player: You're right!

Here are some other things you might ask
about the person:

What book is this person?

What car . . .	What kind of movie . . .
What country . . .	What mineral . . .
What dessert . . .	What part of the body . . .
What facial feature . . .	What piece of furniture . . .
What flower . . .	What recreational event . . .
What fruit . . .	What restaurant . . .
What kind of dog . . .	What sport . . .
What kind of house . . .	What time of day . . .

*This game is said to have been invented by
actor Anthony Perkins on the set of* Psycho
as a between-takes diversion.

49

35 GUESS THE SPEED

Everyone except the driver shuts their eyes and listens to the car sounds. In a little while the driver asks what speed the car is going. The nearest answer wins.

36 HOT OR COLD

One player selects an object that everyone else can see. The player then reveals one characteristic of that object. They might say, "I see something green." The other players take turns guessing what it is. The first player tells them they are "hot" or "cold" or somewhere in between, such as "warm" or "tepid," or somewhere beyond, such as "burning" or "freezing," depending on how close the guessed object is to the correct object. For example, a player might guess, "Is it that tree?" If the tree is very far from the correct object, the first player might answer, "No. You're ice cold." And so on.

37 HOW FAR?
. . . .

Each player looks off to the horizon and
agrees on a landmark—a tree, a mountain,
a barn. Then each player guesses how many
miles away the landmark is and how long
it will take to get there. When you are
ready to begin, set the odometer and state
the time.

When you arrive at the landmark, check
guesses against the odometer and clock.
The player whose guess is closest wins.

38

IN MY SECRET HIDING PLACE
· · · · · · · · · · · · · ·

The first player silently selects an object and begins this game by saying, "In my secret hiding place I keep something that is _____." (One word describing the object is given.) Then everyone gets to make one guess as to what the object is.

If no one guesses the object, another clue is given: "In my secret hiding place I keep something that is _____ and _____." Then everyone gets another guess. New clues are given in this manner until the object is guessed.

39 PICK A NUMBER

. . . .

One player thinks of a number between 1 and 100. The other players try to guess the number by asking questions that may be answered yes or no. For example, the player might have the number 17 in mind. The other players might ask, "Is the number greater than 50?" The answer would be no. The players might then ask, "Is it less than 20?" The answer would be yes. The questions continue until the answer is guessed.

Did you know that you have just practiced deductive reasoning? If you really want to impress your car companions, tell them that in seven guesses you can guess any number they select between 1 and 100. How to do this is revealed on page 113.

40 TRAFFIC LIGHTS

. . . .

Each player guesses how many traffic lights your car will be able to go through without having to stop. The winner is the player who guesses closest. (For obvious reasons, the driver not only doesn't play but is not told the guesses.)

41 TWENTY QUESTIONS

. . . .

One player thinks of a person, place, or thing. The other players try to guess what it is using no more than twenty questions that can be answered yes or no. For younger children, extend the number of questions allowed.

A variation of this game uses animal, vegetable, or mineral categories.

42
WHICH HAND HAS THE PENNY?

One player hides a penny in one hand. The other player tries to guess which hand the penny is in. If the guess is correct, the player earns a point and gets a turn to hide the penny. If the guess is not correct, the first player gets a point and hides the penny again. The winner is the first player to get ten points.

43
WHO AM I?

One player silently selects a famous person whom they would like to be. Players take turns asking questions. For example, if the person selected is Marilyn Monroe, the questions and answers might go something like this:

"Are you a woman?" "Yes."
"Are you living?" "No."
"Did you live in the U.S.?" "Yes."
"Were you a movie star?" "Yes."
"Did you have blond hair?" "Yes."
And so on.

Players may each make three wrong guesses before being eliminated. A time limit of about five or ten minutes is suggested.

44 WINDING ROADS

Each player guesses the color of the next car that will appear from around the next curve in the road. Each correct guess earns a point. The winner is the player with the most points when the road straightens out.

45 IN MY SUITCASE

• • • • • • • • •

The first player says, "I went on a trip and in my suitcase I packed a _____."
The second player continues the game by repeating the sentence completely and adding
another object. Each player continues, always repeating all the old objects and adding a
new object. A player who misses an object or gets them out of order is out. The last
player in the game wins.

Variations of this game include naming objects starting with a particular letter,
or naming objects in alphabetical order. Or you can limit the naming of objects to a
particular category such as Food ("I went to a restaurant and I ordered *pie*.") or Animals
("I went to the zoo and I saw an *antelope*."). Suggestions for more categories are on
page 112.

Make this game easier by not requiring players to repeat all previous objects named.

46 MEMORY BLISS
. . . .

Family members select a past event that they have all shared together: for example, a particular wedding, birthday party, or vacation. Then they take turns remembering a detail of the event.

Mom might say, "I remember when we went to Hana for our vacation. I'm so glad I finally agreed to splurge on renting a red convertible. It was so much fun to ride with the top down."

Dad might add, "I thought it actually worked out well that the trunk was too small to hold all of our suitcases. We wound up putting one upright between you two kids in the back seat, and it helped keep the squabbling down."

A child might add, "I really liked our stops for shave ice and for swimming at the waterfalls. Except I did get scared that a monster might pull me under the water."

Take turns remembering as many more details as possible.

This game is dedicated to my-son-the-film maker, David Meyers, who is the author of a screenplay titled Memory Bliss.

47 WORD CHAINS

· · · · · · · · ·

The first player points out an object and mentions one feature: "There's a *brown* horse." The next player repeats the sentence and adds a one-feature object of their own at the end: "There's a *brown* horse and a *broken* fence." The longer the sentence becomes, the harder it is to remember. A player who makes a mistake is out.

48 BEST ENDING

· · · · · · · · ·

The first player, the narrator, makes up a story lasting two or three minutes and quits telling the story before it is over. Then all the other players take turns making up an ending.

Make the game harder by requiring the narrator to think of a specific ending and then have the other players guess what the ending is.

COUPLETS

Unlike more complicated poems, couplets are very simple. The only rules are that they be two lines long and rhyme. For example:

> My cat is black,
> He sleeps in a sack.

> One, two,
> Buckle your shoe.

> One day my hair turned gray,
> The next day it fell away.

The first player provides the first line, the second player provides the second line.

50

FIVE SENSES POETRY

• • • • • • • • • • •

Make up a poem using all five senses: sight, taste, smell, sound, and touch. As a group, pick a title and then let each person compose a line, or compose lines as a group. For example, using *Vacation* as your title, a poem might go like this:

A vacation is blue.
It tastes like a piña colada.
It smells like salt water.
It sounds like the breaking of waves against the shore.
And it feels like warm sand against my skin.

Make up more poems using any title you desire.

51 RHYMING SLOGANS

Players look for billboards and advertising signs with a one-sentence slogan. For example, a gas station sign might read, "Stop here for gas." The object is to think of a second line that rhymes. In this case, perhaps the second line might be, "And be careful when you pass." This is a good group activity for everyone to work on together.

52 STORY-GO-ROUND

The first player makes up a title for a story. The second player starts the story based on the title. The third continues the story from where the second left off. And so on. Set a time limit for each storyteller of between thirty seconds and one minute. You may also want to set a time by when the story must be completed, or specify that the story is over when everyone has had one or two turns.

If you have access to a tape recorder, it is fun to tape your stories and play them back later.

53 BUZZ
· · · · ·

Players agree on a number between 0 and 9, which will be referred to as the "buzz number." For example, the number 3 might be selected as the buzz number. In round-robin fashion, players take turns counting in numerical sequence, starting with 0. Whenever the buzz number comes up as part of any other number, the player whose turn it is must say "buzz" instead. For example, the first player would say 0, the second would say 1, the third 2, the fourth buzz. The player whose turn it is when the number 13 comes up would again say buzz. And so on. A player who forgets to say buzz at the right time, or says it at the wrong time, is out.

A harder variation of this game uses multiples of a number. For example, if the number is 3, then 6 (2 x 3), 9 (3 x 3), and 12 (4 x 3) would also be buzz numbers. Even harder is using both the number and the multiples. Harder yet is selecting a second number, referred to as the "fizz number," to also keep track of.

54

100

. . . . .

The object of this game is to be the first player to reach 100. Starting with 0, each player takes turns adding any number from 1 to 10. For example, the first player might start with 5. The next player might add 6 for a total of 11, saying aloud both the number and the total. The next player might add 10 for a total of 21. The game continues until someone reaches exactly 100. (You know you are a winner when it's your turn and the current total is between 90 and 99.)

55

TRAVEL MATH PROBLEM

The Jones family leaves Los Angeles heading for New York City driving 60 miles per hour. The Smith family leaves New York City heading for Los Angeles driving at a slower 40 miles per hour. Both families are traveling on the same route. When they meet, who is farther from Los Angeles?

(Answer is on page 113.)

56 TRICKY MATH
· · · · · · · · ·

1. Ask another player to think of a number. Then tell them to:
   • double it
   • add an even number to the answer, telling you what the even number is
   • halve the answer
   • subtract the original number
   Now you can tell them what their final answer is.

2. Ask another player to think of a number. Then tell them to:
   • multiply it by 3
   • add 6
   • divide by 3 and tell you the answer
   Now you can tell them what their original number was.

(The way to do these tricks is revealed on page 114.)

57

CURRENCY EXCHANGE
• • • • • • • • • • •

Players are given the name of a country, and must name that country's currency. This works best if one player names the country and checks the answer.

Argentina	Colombia	Ireland	Poland
Australia	Denmark	Italy	Portugal
Austria	France	Japan	Russia
Belgium	Germany	Mexico	Singapore
Brazil	Greece	Netherlands	Spain
Britain	Hong Kong	Norway	Sweden
Canada	Iceland	Peru	Switzerland
China	India	Philippines	Thailand

Can you name more?

(Answers are on page 114.)

58 GEOGRAPHY
· · · · · · · ·

The first player names a city, state, country, island, body of water, or mountain. The next player names a place that begins with the last letter of the place named. Places may not be repeated. For spelling purposes, words such as *island, river,* and *mountain* are not counted. Nor are *the* and *an.* For example, the first player might name *Albany.* The second player might then name *Yucatan.* The third player might name *the Nile.* And so on. If the game bogs down, set a time limit for a response.

After you have played this game for a while, there is a tendency to run out of names beginning with E or A. At that point you may want to change the rules to drop an ending E or A and use the letter that comes just before it.

Make this game more difficult by limiting it to just cities, or states, or countries. Alter the game by using the same format but a different category. For category suggestions, see page 112.

59 STATE CAPITALS
. . . .

How many state capitals can you name? How many state postal abbreviations can you name? This is harder than you might think! Instead of playing as individuals or teams, consider having the whole family work together to see how many they know as a group. With practice, you'll all become more familiar with the correct answers. You will need one person to check the answers.

Alabama	Indiana	Nebraska	South Carolina
Alaska	Iowa	Nevada	South Dakota
Arizona	Kansas	New Hampshire	Tennessee
Arkansas	Kentucky	New Jersey	Texas
California	Louisiana	New Mexico	Utah
Colorado	Maine	New York	Vermont
Connecticut	Maryland	North Carolina	Virginia
Delaware	Massachusetts	North Dakota	Washington
Florida	Michigan	Ohio	West Virginia
Georgia	Minnesota	Oklahoma	Wisconsin
Hawaii	Mississippi	Oregon	Wyoming
Idaho	Missouri	Pennyslvania	
Illinois	Montana	Rhode Island	

(Answers are on page 114.)

71

60 SUPERLATIVE GEOGRAPHY QUIZ

· · · · · · · · · · · · · ·

1. What is the **longest** river in the world? What continent is it on?
2. Which U.S. states are the **farthest** north, east, west, and south?
3. What is the **oldest** continuously inhabited city, as well as the **oldest** capital city, in the world?
4. What is the **highest** capital city in Europe?
5. What city has the **largest** library in the world?
6. What is the **lowest** point in the former U.S.S.R.?
7. What was the **largest** empire in history?
8. Which continent has the **lowest** average annual rainfall?
9. Which is the world's **largest** continent?
10. What is the **deepest** lake in the United States?

(Answers are on page 115.)

61 TRAVELING
· · · · · · · · ·

One player silently selects a travel destination from anywhere in the world. Taking turns, the other players try to guess what it is with questions that can be answered yes or no. When players think they know the answer, they may guess. If wrong, they are eliminated from that round of the game. If right, they choose the next destination.

62 WONDERS OF THE WORLD
· · · · · · · · · · · · · ·

A. What are the seven natural wonders of the world?
   Can you name the country each is in?

B. What are the seven ancient wonders of the world?
   Can you name the country each was in?
   Can you name the only one that is still standing?

(Answers are on page 115.)

63 HUG BUG

· · · · · · · ·

Even very young children can spot a Volkswagen "beetle." In this game the first player who spots a VW beetle and says "Hug Bug" plus the color of the car (for example, if the car is green, "Hug Bug green") gets to hug the other players.

A variation of this game is to play Slug Bug. The winner then gets to "slug" (nudge gently!) the other players. Yet more variations are the Cadillac Whack, the Truck Buck, and the Continental Shuffle.

64 MAKE A FACE

· · · · · · · · ·

Players name an emotion, then take turns making a face expressing that emotion. Here are some emotions to get you started:

scared	jittery
frustrated	unsure
sad	happy
bored	shy
surprised	suspicious
angry	mad
perplexed	jealous

Can you name more emotions?

65

PANTOMIMES

· · · · · · · ·

The first player silently selects an everyday activity to act out: getting up in the morning, eating an apple, or watching a tennis game, for example. The other players take turns guessing what is going on. The player who guesses correctly acts out the next pantomime.

66

SCISSORS, PAPER, AND STONE
• • • • • • • • • • • • • • •

This is a sign language game.

To make **scissors**, hold your index and middle fingers open in a V.
To make **paper**, hold your hand flat, palm down.
To make **stone**, make a fist.

Two people play at a time. Facing each other, they hold their right hands behind their backs. Each decides which sign they are going to make but does not tell the other. Together they count to three. On the count of three, they both put their right hands out making the sign they have decided upon.

Scissors win over paper, because they can cut it.
Paper wins over stone, because it can cover it.
Stone wins over scissors, because it can blunt them.

If both players choose the same sign, it is a draw and doesn't count. Do this ten times to decide a winner.

67 SECRET FINGER MESSAGES

The first player thinks of a word. The second player closes their eyes, and then the first player uses his or her own index finger to trace each letter of the word on the second person's palm. After a letter is guessed correctly, the second player closes their palm to "erase" and get ready for the next letter.

68

SIMON DOES
· · · · · · · ·

The first player performs a physical activity such as clapping hands. The second player repeats that activity and then adds one of their own. For example, the second player would clap hands and then, perhaps, fake a sneeze. The third player would then clap hands, fake a sneeze, and maybe slap their knees. And so on, until a player forgets one of the activities and is declared out. The game continues until just one player is left.

69 SLAP, SLAP; CLAP, CLAP; SNAP, SNAP
. . . .

For this rhythm game players select a category. (See page 112 for category suggestions.)
Then using a one-two-three rhythm, all players together first slap their thighs twice, then
clap their hands twice, then snap their fingers twice. The first player says the word they have
thought of from the selected category at the same time everyone is snapping their fingers.
Play continues with everyone taking their turn in order. A player who repeats a name or gets
mixed up is out. If the category is States, the game might go something like this:

First player: slap, slap;   Next player: slap, slap;
                   clap, clap;   clap; clap;
                   snap, snap/"Oregon"   snap, snap/"Florida"

And so on.

Make this game harder by requiring that words be added in alphabetical order.

70 COLORED LIGHTS

• • • • • • • • •

The object of this game is for each player to find six different colors of illuminated lights in this order:

> yellow
> orange
> red
> green
> blue
> white

Any player who sees a car with one headlight burned out may skip the color they are looking for and begin looking for the next one.

71 POPEYE

• • • • • • •

Players look for cars with one headlight burned out. When they find one, the first player to say "Popeye" wins a point.

72 DREAM CARS
· · · · · · ·

Players each name their favorite car. Then the first one to spot his or her own favorite wins.

Make this game more difficult by specifying a favorite color, too.

73 FORBIDDEN WORD
· · · · · · · · · · ·

All players agree on a word that they may not say during regular conversation for the next 10 (15, 20) minutes or miles. The word should be common, such as *I, you, yes,* or *car.* Whenever a player says that word and is caught, he or she gets a penalty point. In this case the player with the fewest points at the end wins.

Make this game harder by selecting several forbidden words.

74 I SPY
· · · · ·

All players agree on the object they will be looking for. The first person to spot it says, "I spy!" and wins a point. And so on.

Here are some things you might look for:

> a car with an out-of-state license plate
> a particular make of car
> a black-and-white cow
> a particular breed of dog
> a red flower
> a woman wearing a blue skirt
> a man holding a cane
> a church with a tall steeple
> a galloping horse

Keep the items simple, as players might become frustrated if objects are extremely difficult to find.

75

MILES OF SMILES
· · · · · · · · · ·

All players smile their biggest smiles at people in the cars next to them as they are passing. See how many people you can get to smile back. Waving is OK, too. Making faces isn't.

I take credit for inventing this game, but I'm sure many others have re-invented it—as I probably did, too.

76

QUIET GAME

. . . .

Players agree to see who can be the quietest for the longest. You might also specify a period of time (5 or 10 minutes) or a number of miles.

A variation of this game has players selecting a rarely seen object. Then, none of the players may talk until the object is seen. Suggested objects include a moving train, a cement-mixer truck, a reclining horse, and so on.

A variation of this variation permits only whispering until the object is seen, or using only hand signs and body language.

As is noted in this book's dedication, this game was invented by Jeffrey Feiffer as entertainment for the noisy, restless children in the Meyers family.

77

RACING RAINDROPS

Play this game during a light rain, or just after the rain stops. Looking out their own window, each player picks a raindrop near the top of the window. One player says, "Go!" and then each player tracks their drop until it reaches the bottom of the window. The player whose drop gets to the bottom first is the winner. If a drop should blend with another drop, it is still the player's drop. If two players use the same window, be sure to leave plenty of space between the racing drops.

RECIPE DETECTIVES
• • • • • • • • • • •

Each player names an item that they like to eat, and then names the ingredients used in the recipe. For example, if a player names "chocolate chip cookies" the appropriate ingredients would be flour, sugar, eggs, butter, vanilla, chocolate chips, and nuts. However, when this game is played with younger children, or older children and adults who are not familiar with cooking, the ingredient suggestions can sometimes be quite humorous. Players get one point (or one cookie, cracker, raisin, etc.) per correct ingredient named. The family cook(s) may provide clues, settle disputes, and pass along valuable information.

This game originated in the Meyers family car as I passed out some homemade chocolate chip cookies. Curiosity about the ingredients developed into this game, which has become quite popular with family members.

79 SAFETY SPIES

· · · · · · · ·

Each player looks for unsafe conduct by pedestrians and drivers. When an unsafe act is spotted, the player points it out. After a family discussion that verifies the act was dangerous, the player gets a point.

80 SECRET WORD

· · · · · · · · ·

Each player chooses a noun and tells the other players what it is. Then turn on the car radio. The first player to hear their word spoken wins. It's sort of like when the duck dropped down on Groucho Marx's TV show *You Bet Your Life.*

81 STRAIGHT FACE
· · · · · · · · · ·

All but the first player decide on a phrase that the first player must use in answer to any question they are asked—without laughing. For instance, the phrase might be "a one-eyed, one-toed flying purple people-eater." The others might ask, "What is your favorite breakfast cereal?" or "What object do you need to play your favorite game?" And so on, to which the first player must always answer, "A one-eyed, one-toed flying purple people-eater." When the first player laughs, it is another player's turn. This game works best with very young children.

82  FIVE WORDS
• • • • • • • • •

In this activity you say five words that describe yourself. Taking turns, the other players then each add another word that they think describes you. After some discussion, the next player takes a turn.

83

PERSONAL FAVORITES
• • • • • • • • • • •

Learn more about your traveling companions with this enticing game. Ask each person these questions:

What is your favorite song? Why? How much of it can you sing? Sing it now.

What is your favorite sport? Why?

What is your favorite animal? Why?

What is your favorite TV show? Why?

What is your favorite holiday? Why?

What is your favorite day of the week? Why?

What is your favorite subject in school? Why?

What was your favorite birthday celebration? Why?

What is your favorite dessert? What are some of the ingredients used to make it?

What is your favorite color? What things do you own in that color?

What is your favorite joke? Tell it now.

What is your favorite form of transportation? Why?

You can also ask about the person's favorite

movie star	flower	book
singing star	friend	tree
food	outfit	number
game	restaurant	name
holiday	hobby	pet

Can you think of more things to ask about?

A variation of this game is to ask about *least* favorites. Or turn this into a guessing game by having everyone guess the answer a particular person would give. That person then verifies the answer.

84

TIME TRAVEL
• • • • • • • •

Each player answers
these questions:

- If you could travel
  back in time, which
  period would you
  choose? Why?
- Would you rather
  travel forward in
  time? If so, why?

85

WHAT IF . . .
. . . .

In this activity, each person answers these questions:

- What if a genie appeared and granted you three wishes?
  What would you wish for?

- What if you won a million dollars?
  What would you spend it on?

- What if you could be an animal?
  What kind of animal would you be? Why?

- What if you could travel anywhere?
  Where would you go? Why?

- What if you could have any pet?
  What would you pick?

86 ADAGES

· · · · · · ·

Adages are old sayings that are popularly accepted as truths. Can you complete these familiar sayings? Can you explain what they mean? (Adults may be able to help with explanations.)

1. Don't count your chickens . . .

2. A bird in the hand is worth . . .

3. Don't put the cart before . . .

4. Sometimes you can't see the forest for the . . .

5. People who live in glass houses shouldn't . . .

6. There's no point in crying over . . .

7. One picture is worth a . . .

8. A rolling stone gathers . . .

9. Birds of a feather . . .

10. You can't make a silk purse out of a . . .

11. Every cloud has a . . .

12. You can't teach an old dog . . .

13. You reap what . . .

14. The early bird gets . . .

15. He who wants too much . . .

16. Slow and steady wins . . .

17. A stitch in time . . .

18. Better late than . . .

19. United we stand, divided . . .

20. Early to bed, early to rise, makes a man . . .

21. One picture is worth a . . .

22. All that glitters . . .

23. All's well that . . .

24. Curiosity killed . . .

25. Don't burn your bridges . . .

26. Where there's a will . . .

27. Waste not . . .

28. Haste makes . . .

29. A fool and his money are . . .

30. You can't have your cake and . . .

31. Too many cooks . . .

32. Strike while the . . .

33. A watched pot . . .

34. Look before . . .

35. Don't put all your eggs . . .

36. Ignorance is . . .

(Answers are on page 116.)

87 ANIMAL GROUPS

. . . .

How many of these collective nouns for animal groups can you name?

1. A (flock) of birds
2. A ? of lions
3. A ? of rhinos
4. A ? of geese
5. A ? of ants
6. A ? of buffalo
7. A ? of sheep
8. A ? of wolves
9. A ? of fish
10. A ? of bees
11. A ? of turtles
12. A ? of bats
13. A ? of baby bats

14. A ? of bachelor dolphins
15. A ? of whales
16. A ? of hyenas
17. A ? of frogs
18. A ? of baboons
19. A ? of hippopotamuses
20. A ? of eagles
21. A ? of sparrows
22. A ? of starlings

Can you think of more animal groups?

(Answers are on page 116.)

NAME SANTA'S REINDEER
· · · · · · · · · · · · · · · · ·

Can you name Santa's nine
reindeer?

(Answers are on page 117.)

NAME THE COLONIES
· · · · · · · · · · · · ·

Can you name the thirteen
original American colonies?

(Answers are on page 117.)

90 NAME THE DWARFS

• • • • • • • • •

A. Can you name Snow White's seven dwarfs?

B. Which of the seven dwarfs doesn't have a beard?

(Answers are on page 117.)

91 NAME THE PLANETS

• • • • • • • • •

A. Name the nine planets, starting with the one closest to the sun.

B. What is the name of the star that is closest to Earth?

(Answers are on page 117.)

92

NAME THE TEN COMMANDMENTS AND THE SEVEN DEADLY SINS

• • • • • • • • • • •

A. What are the Ten Commandments?

B. What are the seven deadly sins?

(Answers are on pages 117 and 118.)

93

NAME THE U.S. PRESIDENTS

• • • • • • • • • •

How many of the U.S. presidents can you name? How many can you name in sequential order, beginning with the first president?

(Answers are on page 118.)

94 OFFICIAL INITIALS

· · · · · · · · · · ·

Players take turns telling what
these initials stand for:

1. A.A.
2. A.M.
3. A.S.A.P.
4. C.B.S.
5. C.O.D.
6. E.S.P.
7. F.B.I.
8. I.O.U.
9. I.R.S.

10. M.P.H.
11. P.D.Q.
12. P.M.
13. R.P.M.
14. R.S.V.P.
15. T.G.I.F.
16. T.V.
17. U.S.A.F.

Can you name more?

(Answers are on page 118.)

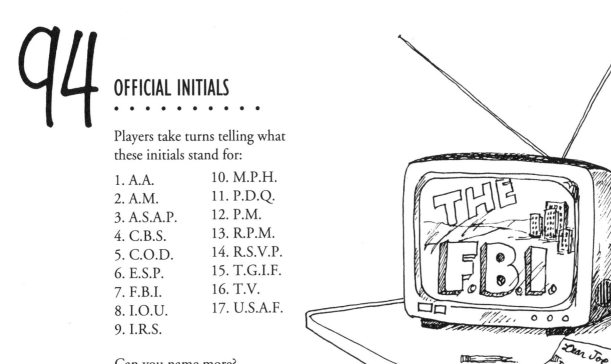

95

KNOCK KNOCK JOKES
· · · · · · · · · ·

Knock Knock.
Who's there?
Midas.
Midas who?
Midas well relax—we're on vacation!

· · ·

Knock Knock.
Who's there?
Datsun.
Datsun who?
Datsun awful joke.

· · ·

Knock Knock.
Who's there?
Eiffel.
Eiffel who?
Eiffel off my horse.

Knock Knock.
Who's there?
Mandy.
Mandy who?
Mandy lifeboats! Our ship is sinking!

· · ·

Knock Knock.
Who's there?
Water skier.
Water skier who?
Water skier'd of? I'm harmless.

· · ·

Knock Knock.
Who's there?
Boo.
Boo who?
Don't cry! It's only a joke!

Can you think of more Knock Knock jokes?

103

96 TONGUE TWISTERS

How many times can you say these tongue twisters without tangling your tongue?

- Toy boat.
- Peter Piper picked a peck of pickled peppers. How many peppers did Peter Piper pick?
- Round the rugged rocks the ragged rascal ran.
- She sells seashells on the seashore.
- How much wood could a woodchuck chuck, if a woodchuck could chuck wood?
- Black bug's blood.
- Leon the lovable llama licked lollipops in Lima.
- Troy tasted tangy tarts two at a time.
- Unique New York.
- Tina has ten tiny toes.
- Red leather, yellow leather.
- Bonnie bought both boats.

Can you say these tongue twisters just once?

- Stop chop shops selling chopped shop chops.
- Crazy Chris crushed the creepy creature with his creature crusher.

These two tongue twisters are particularly popular with children in the stage at which they think toilet humor is hilarious. Be careful!

- One smart fellow, he felt smart.
  Two smart fellows, they felt smart.
  Three smart fellows, they all felt smart.

- She slit a sheet.
  A sheet she slit.
  Upon a slitted sheet she sits.

97 VACATION AND GEOGRAPHY JOKES
. . . .

VACATION JOKES

1. Why did the clock need a vacation?
2. Why did the tire need a vacation?
3. Why wasn't the elephant allowed on the airplane?
4. What is heavier in summer than in winter?
5. Why did the Egyptian mummy go to the resort hotel?
6. What is gray and has four legs and a trunk?
7. What is tan and has four legs and a trunk?
8. What should never be said to a pilot named Jack?
9. What has four legs and flies?
10. What's black and red all over and hates to be touched?

GEOGRAPHY JOKES

11. Where do fish go for a vacation?
12. Where do singing birds go for a vacation?
13. What did Tennessee?
14. What state has only one actor in it?
15. What people travel the most?
16. What people travel the fastest?

(Answers are on page 119.)

VACATION RIDDLES

1. On a car vacation a family rode for three days and didn't get tired. Why?

2. Two travelers were playing checkers. They played five games, and each traveler won the same number of games. How?

3. A family's car was facing west. After driving for several minutes they discovered that they were actually going east. Can you explain this?

4. How did the camper make a fire with only one stick?

(Answers are on page 119.)

99

ANIMAL LIST
· · · · · · · ·

Keep track of all the different animals your family spots during your car trips. Write them down, along with date and location.

Animal	Date	Location
1. _____	_____	_____
2. _____	_____	_____
3. _____	_____	_____
4. _____	_____	_____
5. _____	_____	_____
6. _____	_____	_____

VANITY LICENSE PLATE LOG
. . . .

Keep track of the unusual vanity plates your family spots during car trips.

State _____ Car make_____

Date _____ Time _____

Location _____

State _____ Car make_____

Date _____ Time _____

Location _____

State _____ Car make_____

Date _____ Time _____

Location _____

Can you make up an appropriate
vanity plate for your family's car?

101

UNITED STATES LICENSE PLATE GAME

. . . .

Color in each state on the map of the United States as you spot a license plate from that state. Use the map to answer these questions.

1. Can you find a way to go from the Atlantic Ocean to the Pacific Ocean by going through only seven states? Is there more than one way?

2. Can you find three ways to go from Michigan to Utah by crossing only four other states? Can you name the states?

3. Can you find the two states that border the greatest number of other states? Can you name the states they border?

4. Can you find the two states that have seven neighbors?

5. Can you find the state that touches only one other state?

6. Can you find the two states that don't touch any other states?

7. Can you find the five states that border on the Gulf of Mexico?

8. Can you find the state on the Atlantic Coast that is closest to California?

9. Can you find a way to get from the Pacific Ocean to the Atlantic Ocean by passing through every state only once? (You may not enter either Mexico or Canada, and Hawaii and Alaska are excluded.)

(Answers are on page 119.)

(State capitals are on page 114.)

CATEGORIES

· · · · · · · ·

Animals
Automobiles
Beverages
Bible Characters
Birds
Book Titles
Boys' Names
Buildings
Candies
Car Models
Cartoon Characters
Cats
Celebrities
Cities

Clothing
Cold Things
Colors
Countries
Dogs
Drinks
Feelings
Fish
Flowers
Foods
Friends
Fruits
Furniture
Games

Girls' Names
Hobbies
Hot Things
Landmarks
Magazines
Movies
Movie Stars
Names
Nations
Neighbors
Occupations
Plants
Political Figures
Relatives

Song Titles
Sports Figures
States
Stores
Stories
Storybook Characters
Transportation
Trees
TV Personalities
TV Shows
Vacation Words
Vegetables
Vehicles

ANSWERS
· · · · · · ·

#27. SUPERLATIVES
1. Crater Lake in Oregon
2. the Mississippi
3. the Volga in the former Soviet Union
4. the Nile in Africa
5. Lake Superior in the United States
6. Point Reyes, in California near San Francisco
7. Hawaii
8. California (29 million people)
9. Bad Water, in Death Valley in California
10. Rhode Island

#39. PICK A NUMBER
Always pick the midpoint of the remaining range and then ask if the unknown number is greater than (or less than) that midpoint number. For example, if the unknown number is 17, the questions might go like this:

1. You: Is the number greater than 50 (half of 100)? Answer: No. Remaining range: 1-50.
2. You: Is the number greater than 25 (half of 50)? Answer: No. Remaining range: 1-25.
3. You: Is the number greater than 12 (half of 25)? Answer: Yes. Remaining range: 13-25.
4. You: Is the number greater than 19 (number midway between 13 & 25)? Answer: No. Remaining range: 13-19.
5. You: Is the number greater than 16 (number midway between 13 & 19)? Answer: Yes. Remaining range: 17-19.
6. You: Is the number greater than 18 (number midway between 17 & 19)? Answer: No. Remaining range: 17-18.
7. You: Is the number 18? Answer: No. You: The number is 17!

#55. TRAVEL MATH PROBLEM
1. Neither. When they meet, both families are the same distance from both cities.

#56. TRICKY MATH

1. The final answer will always be half of the even number they gave you.
2. The original number is always two less than the final answer.

#57. CURRENCY EXCHANGE

Argentina (peso)
Australia (dollar)
Austria (schilling)
Belgium (franc)
Brazil (cruzeiro)
Britain (pound)
Canada (dollar)
China (yuan)
Colombia (peso)
Denmark (krone)
France (franc)
Germany (mark)
Greece (drachma)
Hong Kong (dollar)
Iceland (krona)
India (rupee)
Ireland (pound)
Italy (lira)
Japan (yen)
Mexico (peso)
Netherlands (gulder)
Norway (krone)
Peru (sol)
Philippines (peso)
Poland (zloti)
Portugal (escudo)
Russia (ruble)
Singapore (dollar)
Spain (peseta)
Sweden (krona)
Switzerland (franc)
Thailand (baht)

#59. STATE CAPITALS

Alabama (Montgomery) – AL
Alaska (Juneau) – AK
Arizona (Phoenix) – AZ
Arkansas (Little Rock) – AR
California (Sacramento) – CA
Colorado (Denver) – CO
Connecticut (Hartford) – CT
Delaware (Dover) – DE
Florida (Tallahassee) – FL
Georgia (Atlanta) – GA
Hawaii (Honolulu) – HI
Idaho (Boise) – ID
Illinois (Springfield) – IL
Indiana (Indianapolis) – IN
Iowa (Des Moines) – IA
Kansas (Topeka) – KS
Kentucky (Frankfort) – KY
Louisiana (Baton Rouge) – LA
Maine (Augusta) – ME
Maryland (Annapolis) – MD
Massachusetts (Boston) – MA
Michigan (Lansing) – MI
Minnesota (St. Paul) – MN
Mississippi (Jackson) – MS
Missouri (Jefferson City) – MO
Montana (Helena) – MT

Nebraska (Lincoln) – NE
Nevada (Carson City) – NV
New Hampshire (Concord) – NH
New Jersey (Trenton) – NJ
New Mexico (Santa Fe) – NM
New York (Albany) – NY
North Carolina (Raleigh) – NC
North Dakota (Bismarck) – ND
Ohio (Columbus) – OH
Oklahoma (Oklahoma City) – OK
Oregon (Salem) – OR
Pennsylvania (Harrisburg) – PA
Rhode Island (Providence) – RI
South Carolina (Columbia) – SC
South Dakota (Pierre) – SD
Tennessee (Nashville) – TN
Texas (Austin) – TX
Utah (Salt Lake City) – UT
Vermont (Montpelier) – VT
Virginia (Richmond) – VA
Washington (Olympia) – WA
West Virginia (Charleston) – WV
Wisconsin (Madison) – WI
Wyoming (Cheyenne) – WY

#60. SUPERLATIVE GEOGRAPHY QUIZ

1. The Nile; Africa
2. North—Alaska; East—Maine; West—Alaska; South—Hawaii
3. Damascus (in Syria)
4. Madrid (in Spain) at 2,150 feet above sea level
5. Washington, D.C., with the Library of Congress
6. The Caspian Sea at 92 feet below sea level
7. The Mongol Empire
8. Antarctica
9. Asia
10. Crater Lake in Oregon

#62. WONDERS OF THE WORLD

A. 1. Great Barrier Reef (Australia)
   2. Painted Caves (France and Spain)
   3. Rio De Janeiro Harbor (Brazil)
   4. Paricutin Volcano (Mexico)
   5. Grand Canyon (United States)
   6. Victoria Falls (Africa)
   7. Mount Everest (on the border between Nepal and Tibet in Asia)

B. 1. Great Pyramid at Giza (Egypt)
   2. Walls and Hanging Gardens of Babylon (Iraq)
   3. Colossus of Rhodes (Greece)
   4. Mausoleum of Halicarnassus (Greece)
   5. Temple of Artemis at Ephesus (Greece)
   6. Statue of Zeus at Olympia (Greece)
   7. Pharos (lighthouse) of Alexandria (Egypt)

The Great Pyramid still stands. It remains the largest stone building in the world.

#86. ADAGES

1. before they hatch.
2. two in the bush.
3. the horse.
4. trees.
5. throw stones.
6. spilled milk.
7. thousand words.
8. no moss.
9. flock together.
10. sow's ear.
11. silver lining.
12. new tricks.
13. you sow.
14. the worm.
15. loses all.
16. the race.
17. saves nine.
18. never.
19. we fall.
20. healthy, wealthy, and wise.
21. thousand words.
22. is not gold.
23. ends well.
24. the cat.
25. behind you.
26. there's a way.
27. want not.
28. waste.
29. soon parted.
30. eat it too.
31. spoil the broth.
32. iron is hot.
33. never boils.
34. you leap.
35. in one basket.
36. bliss.

#87. ANIMAL GROUPS

2. A (pride) of lions
3. A (crash) of rhinos
4. A (gaggle) of geese
5. A (covey) of ants
6. A (herd) of buffalo
7. A (flock) of sheep
8. A (pack) of wolves
9. A (school) of fish
10. A (swarm) of bees
11. A (rafter) of turtles
12. A (colony) of bats
13. A (creche) of baby bats
14. A (coalition) of bachelor dolphins
15. A (pod) of whales
16. A (clan) of hyenas
17. An (army) of frogs
18. A (troop) of baboons
19. A (school) of hippopotamuses
20. A (convocation) of eagles
21. A (host) of sparrows
22. A (chattering) of starlings

#88. NAME SANTA'S REINDEER

1. Dasher
2. Dancer
3. Prancer
4. Vixen
5. Comet
6. Cupid
7. Donner
8. Blitzen
9. Rudolph

#89. NAME THE COLONIES

1. Virginia
2. Maryland
3. Massachusetts
4. Connecticut
5. New Hampshire
6. Rhode Island
7. New York
8. New Jersey
9. Delaware
10. Pennsylvania
11. North Carolina
12. South Carolina
13. Georgia

#90. NAME THE DWARFS

A. 1. Dopey
   2. Sleepy
   3. Doc
   4. Grumpy
   5. Happy
   6. Sneezy
   7. Bashful

B. Dopey does not have a beard.

#91. NAME THE PLANETS

A. 1. Mercury
   2. Venus
   3. Earth
   4. Mars
   5. Jupiter
   6. Saturn
   7. Uranus
   8. Neptune
   9. Pluto
B. the sun

#92. NAME THE TEN COMMANDMENTS AND THE SEVEN DEADLY SINS

A. 1. Thou shalt have no other gods before me.
   2. Thou shalt not make unto thee any graven image.
   3. Thou shalt not take the name of the Lord thy God in vain.
   4. Remember the Sabbath day, to keep it holy.
   5. Honor thy father and thy mother.
   6. Thou shalt not kill.
   7. Thou shalt not commit adultery.
   8. Thou shalt not steal.

9. Thou shalt not bear false witness against thy neighbor.
10. Thou shalt not covet thy neighbor's house.

(Note that in different Bible versions the Ten Commandments vary slightly in wording and order.)

B. 1. pride (or vanity)
2. covetousness (or greed)
3. lust
4. anger
5. gluttony
6. envy
7. sloth

#93. NAME THE U.S. PRESIDENTS
1. George Washington
2. John Adams
3. Thomas Jefferson
4. James Madison
5. James Monroe
6. John Quincy Adams
7. Andrew Jackson
8. Martin Van Buren
9. William H. Harrison
10. John Tyler
11. James K. Polk
12. Zachary Taylor
13. Millard Fillmore
14. Franklin Pierce
15. James Buchanan
16. Abraham Lincoln
17. Andrew Johnson
18. Ulysses S. Grant
19. Rutherford B. Hayes
20. James A. Garfield
21. Chester A. Arthur
22. Grover Cleveland
23. Benjamin Harrison
24. Grover Cleveland
25. William McKinley
26. Theodore Roosevelt
27. William H. Taft
28. Woodrow Wilson
29. Warren G. Harding
30. Calvin Coolidge
31. Herbert C. Hoover
32. Franklin D. Roosevelt
33. Harry S. Truman
34. Dwight D. Eisenhower
35. John F. Kennedy
36. Lyndon B. Johnson
37. Richard M. Nixon
38. Gerald R. Ford
39. James E. Carter
40. Ronald W. Reagan
41. George Bush

#94. OFFICIAL INITIALS
1. Alcoholics Anonymous
2. ante meridiem: before the sun meets the meridian
3. as soon as possible
4. Central Broadcasting System
5. cash on delivery
6. extrasensory perception
7. Federal Bureau of Investigation
8. I owe you
9. Internal Revenue Service

10. miles per hour
11. pretty darn quick
12. post meridiem: after the sun meets the meridian
13. revolutions per minute
14. Originally a French phrase, "Repondez, s'il vous plait," this abbreviation has translated into English as, "Respond (or Reply) soon via post (or, nowadays, phone)."
15. Thank God it's Friday!
16. television
17. United States Air Force

#97. VACATION AND GEOGRAPHY JOKES

1. It was all wound up.
2. It couldn't take the pressure any more.
3. Because its trunk wouldn't fit under the seat.
4. Traffic to the beach.
5. It needed to unwind.
6. A mouse going on vacation.
7. A mouse returning from vacation.
8. "Hi, Jack!"
9. A picnic table.
10. A sunburned zebra.
11. Finland.
12. The Canary Islands.
13. The same thing Arkansas.
14. Texas (the Lone Star State).
15. The Romans.
16. The Russians.

#98. VACATION RIDDLES

1. They slept at night.
2. They played different people.
3. The car was in reverse gear.
4. It was a match.

#101. UNITED STATES LICENSE PLATE GAME

1. GA-TN-AR-OK-NM-AZ-CA. Yes: start alternatively in either NC or VA.
2. WI-MN-SD-WY; WI-IA-NE-WY; WI-IA-NE-CO.
3. Missouri (IA, NE, KS, OK, AR, TN, KY, IL) and Tennessee (MO, AR, MS, AL, GA, NC, VA, KY).
4. Colorado and Kentucky.
5. Maine.
6. Alaska and Hawaii.
7. Alabama, Florida, Louisiana, Mississippi, and Texas.
8. Georgia.
9. One way to do this follows this route: WA, OR, CA, NV, ID, UT, AZ, NM, CO, WY, MT, ND, MN, SD, NE, KS, OK, TX, LA, AR, MO, IA, WI, MI, IN, IL, KY, TN, MS, AL, FL, GA, SC, NC, VA, WV, OH, PA, MD, DE, NJ, NY, CT, RI, MA, VT, NH, ME.

AGE RECOMMENDATIONS

· · · · · · · · · · · · · · · ·

These lists categorize the games and activities in this book according to the age of the youngest child who may fully participate. Use the categories only as a quick reference. Because of individual differences, some preschoolers are capable of playing and enjoying a game recommended for older children. And some older children enjoy playing simpler games, especially if they are playing with a younger sibling.

Game numbers are in parentheses.

FOR PRESCHOOLERS

· · · · · · · · ·

Animal List (#99)
Best Ending (#48)
Colored Lights (#70)
Dream Cars (#72)
Hot or Cold (#36)

Hug Bug (#63)
In My Secret Hiding Place (#38)
I Spy (#74)
Make a Face (#64)
Miles of Smiles (#75)
Name Santa's Reindeer (#88)
Noises (#23)
Popeye (#71)
Quiet Game (#76)
Racing Raindrops (#77)
Straight Face (#81)
Superlatives (#27)
Tasty Talk (#29)
What Am I Counting? (#4)
What If . . . (#85)
Which Hand Has the Penny? (#42)
Winding Roads (#44)
Your New Car (#5)

FOR GRADES K-3

· · · · · · · · ·

Alphabets (#13)
Antonyms (#14)

Backwards Spelling Bee (#15)
Bus Stop (#1)
Categories (#16)
Couplets (#49)
Five Words (#82)
Five Ws (#19)
Forbidden Word (#73)
Knock Knock Jokes (#95)
License Plate Alphabet (#6)
License Plate Counting (#7)
License Plate Math (#8)
License Plate Palindromes (#9)
License Plate Phrases (#10)
Memory Bliss (#46)
Mind Your Ps and Qs (#2)
Multiple Meanings (#22)
Name the Dwarfs (#90)
Pantomimes (#65)
Personal Favorites (#83)
Pick a Number (#39)
Pig Latin (#24)
Recipe Detectives (#78)
Rhyming Slogans (#51)

INDEX

• • • • •

Page numbers are at the right.

People who have helped put this book together:

Book Design and Typesetting: Betsy Joyce
Copy Editing: Virginia A. Rich
Game Testing: Debbie and Roger Murray, and sons Greg (age 6) and Doug (age 3)
                        Gene Meyers, and daughter Suzie (age 12)
Printing: McNaughton & Gunn
United States Map (p. 111): Eureka Cartography

ABOUT THE AUTHOR

Carole Terwilliger Meyers holds a B.A. degree in anthropology from San Francisco State University and an elementary teaching credential from Fresno State University. Her articles have appeared in *Family Circle, Parenting, Family Fun, New Choices,* and *San Francisco Focus* magazines, as well as numerous other magazines and newspapers, and she has been a columnist for *California* magazine, *Parents' Press,* the *San Francisco Examiner,* and the *San Jose Mercury News.* Ms. Meyers resides in Berkeley, California with her husband and two children.

Mike Maloney
San Francisco Chronicle

ABOUT THE ILLUSTRATOR

Victoria Carlson is a graduate of the San Francisco Art Institute and currently works at the Oakland Museum. She resides in Oakland, California.

INVITATION TO CONTRIBUTE
· · · · · · · · · · · · ·

Do you have a favorite car game or activity that is not included in this book?
Share it with me, and if I select it to use in *Miles of Smiles II* you'll be given credit as
a contributor and will receive a free copy. I look forward to hearing from you.

Carole Terwilliger Meyers
c/o **Carousel Press**
P.O. Box 6038
Berkeley, CA 94706-0038

MORE GREAT BOOKS FROM CAROUSEL PRESS

• •

THE FAMILY TRAVEL GUIDE: AN INSPIRING COLLECTION OF FAMILY-FRIENDLY VACATIONS

These meaty tales from the trenches promise to help you avoid some of the pitfalls of traveling with children. Information is included on hot spots of family travel (California, Hawaii, Washington D.C., Europe) as well as on lesser-touted havens (Las Vegas, New York City, Belize, Jamaica), and how-to-do-it details are provided on home-exchanging, RVing, selecting souvenirs, and traveling with teens. A comprehensive bibliography annotates travel guides and travel-related children's literature currently in print. *432 pages. $16.95.*

THE ZOO BOOK: A GUIDE TO AMERICA'S BEST

Detailed descriptions of the top 53 U.S. zoos are included. The author has visited each zoo, and his review includes hours and admission fees, driving and bus directions, don't-miss exhibits, touring tips to make a visit easier and more efficient, and details on the entertainment available. Each zoo's featured exhibits are highlighted—plus other exhibits are described, special attractions for the kids are noted, and what's new at the zoo is discussed. Smaller zoos, aquariums, and other places that display animals are also described, as are noteworthy zoos in Canada, Mexico, Europe, and other areas of the world. An entire chapter is devoted to descriptions and photos of interesting zoo animals. *288 pages. $14.95.*

WEEKEND ADVENTURES IN NORTHERN CALIFORNIA

The vacation riches of Northern California are detailed—including the San Francisco Bay Area, the Gold Rush country, ski resorts, and family camps. This guide covers where to stay, where to eat, and what to do and also provides appropriate information for families—such as the availability of highchairs, booster seats, and cribs. Don't leave home without it! *416 pages. $17.95.*

DREAM SLEEPS: CASTLE & PALACE HOTELS OF EUROPE

Designed to make fairy tales come true, this book details the exciting castles and palaces in Europe that are open to the public for lodging and dining. Using the positioning maps included for each country, you can easily determine which hotels potentially fit your itinerary. All information needed to make an informed decision (driving instructions, rates, food service, family amenities, on-site recreation, nearby diversions) is included along with the basic phone and fax numbers and U.S. booking representatives. The author, who has personally visited each hotel, includes a fascinating history for each and an enticing description of the present-day facilities. *304 pages. $17.95.*